Gentil

Nice things in life that don't cost anything

Noel Denvir

Bloomington, IN  Milton Keynes, UK

authorHOUSE®

AuthorHouse™
1663 Liberty Drive,
Suite 200
Bloomington, IN 47403
www.authorhouse.com
Phone: 1-800-839-8640

AuthorHouse™ *UK Ltd.*
500 Avebury Boulevard
Central Milton Keynes, MK9 2BE
www.authorhouse.co.uk
Phone: 08001974150

            1/27/2007
First published by AuthorHouse
ISBN: 978-1-4259-5822-0 (sc)

Printed in the United States of America
Bloomington, Indiana

<u>GENTIL</u> stands for:
God Everyday Nice Things In Life.

It is a collection of observations, incidents, perceptions and feelings which make up the miniature theatre of our daily lives.

They are things that we will all recognize but perhaps have never really focussed on. It is about seeing the extraordinary in the ordinary.

<u>DENTIL</u> stands for:
Devil Everyday Niggly Things In Life.

Although focussing on more negative experiences, it does offer reassurance in highlighting things that happen to us all.

There are 1,300 Gentils and 500 Dentils in this book.

I hope they will make you think and smile.

Table of Contents

GENTILS

DENTILS

GENTILS

Gentil 1.

1. The first glimpse of the
    sea after a long drive.

2. Reservoir dams.

3. Amusing alternative meanings
    to well-known abbreviations.

4. Raising your arms above your
    head in a kitchen where things are
    cooking and feeling the warm air.

5. After driving out of the city:
    getting out of the car and taking
    that first breath of country air.

6. A light on in a house late at night.

7. Waking up one morning after a
    bout of illness and feeling better.

8. Floodlit public buildings.

9.   Seeing the resemblance of
     a friend in their child.

10. Comic versions of well-known songs.

11. Developing an affection
     for another town.

12. The small, illuminated area
     around a streetlamp.

13. Arabic and Oriental writing.

14. Blowing across the top of
     an empty bottle to make a
     deep, whistling sound.

15. Blowing up a balloon and
     then letting it go, so that it
     blubbers all over the room.

16. Holding yourself straight,
     and then falling backwards
     into the arms of a friend.

17. The harmless kleptomania of
     stealing little bars of soap or
     sugar sachets from a hotel.

18. Discovering an interesting new fact.

19. The vapour clouds from people's mouths when they breathe out on cold mornings.

20. Bookends.

21. The hypnotic gaze of a person reading a morning newspaper.

22. Twins.

23. Sparks.

24. The glow of a city in a night sky.

25. The little rush of pleasure you get when a child says something sweet.

26. How a familiar tune sounds even better in a movie.

27. The sound of footsteps on pebbles.

28. The names of very small villages.

29. The witty or dramatic second title that major films are given.

30. The strange little strokes and squiggles that one finds in Scandinavian languages.

31. When a woman puts both hands to the back of her neck and flicks her long hair out.

32. When a person grabs the thumb of one hand with the other, then moves to the other fingers of that hand in order to count off a list of important points.

33. A photo series of a tree or landscape taken at different times of the year.

34. The gradual change that you notice has happened, but which you never actually see happening, like the movement of the hour hand of a clock.

35. Waking up one morning and seeing a snow-covered landscape.

36. Using the short space of time created by a long traffic light or traffic jam to do some tidying up in the car.

37. Drinking from water-filled, cupped hands.

38. The little safety drill dance that the flight attendants do before take-off.

39. Cool words like:"Plate Techtonics".

40. Chimney smoke.

41. Throwing a sweet or nut in the air and catching it in your mouth.

42. A wrinkled and dog-eared reference book that looks twenty times its age because of exhaustive and loving use.

43. Alcoves.

44. Woolly hats that go over your ears.

45. Sliding in your socks across a shiny wooden floor.

46. Belgian comics.

47. Large, foreign postage stamps.

48. The former names of
     African countries.

49. How, regardless of your age, actors
     like Humphrey Bogart always
     seem to be older than you.

50. Motorbikes with sidecars.

51. Someone asking you where you
     bought this delicious cake.

52. The faces men pull when
     they are shaving.

53. Old units of measurement
     like leagues and bushels.

54. People with surnames that
     suit their professions.

55. Ingenious little household
     tips for cleaning things.

56. The light, humming sound
     that people make when they're
     eating something delicious.

57. People who have the same
    job, status or study as you,
    and so doing, occupy a
    fascinating parallel universe.

58. The sound of your PC when
    you're peacefully surfing or
    looking through your emails.

59. Palindromes.

60. Photos of loved ones.

61. Pressing cold hands onto a radiator.

62. The chance to observe someone you
    love when they're not looking.

63. Doing something really
    stupid, and then being able to
    laugh about it afterwards.

64. The rustle of leaves.

65. Being kissed in direct sunlight.

66. Finally seeing a place that you'd
    only ever studied on a map before.

67. The various victory dances that footballers do after scoring a goal.

68. Finally getting around to doing that little repair job you've been promising to do for ages.

69. The very idea of castanets.

70. The way everyone jumps when a mobile phone rings.

71. A smell that instantly reminds you of your childhood.

72. Looking up the details about a piece of world news that happened when you were a child, and then understanding it better as an adult.

73. Driving past a hedgerow at a speed that enables you to see through it.

74. Branches swaying in the wind.

75. Something that stays inherently clean, like the inside of a washing machine.

76. Using a bag to store bags in.

77. People on stilts.

78. Steamy kitchen windows.

79. Hanging streetlamps that sway in the wind at night.

80. Opening a large window.

81. Seeing someone in a fit of laughter.

82. Hearing a bilingual child switch languages.

83. Using small household objects, such as a salt cellar or a cigarette packet, to reconstruct a miniature layout of a place you want to describe to someone;then seeing them examining the model as if it were the real thing.

84. The smell of the sea telling you that you're near the coast.

85. A passerby who is still smiling at a joke they heard.

86. The classroom smell of pencil
    sharpeners and sandwiches.

87. A music student with a
    cello case on her back.

88. The look on a person's face listening
    to the details of your operation.

89. When two dogs get stuck together.

90. When the inside cover of a book
    and its first page are the same
    dark and impressive colour.

91. Cutting a large, fresh tomato
    with a sharp, serrated knife.

92. Real lettering.

93. Little pieces of information
    or facts that you decide

to believe without any particular rationale.

94. Standing on tiptoe.

95. Anecdotes.

96. Highly skilled and specialized professions like musical instrument making or roof thatching.

97. Saddles.

98. Church organs.

99. Writing with a fountain pen.

100. The relief when someone speaks an embarrassing truth that everyone understands.

Gentil 2.

1. The truck driver and his young son who has come along for the day.

2. A heart-lifting display of good manners.

3. Those unmanned space probes that travel through space for decades.

4. Bonsai trees.

5. Seeing the little bubbles rise from your bicycle inner tube immersed in water, indicating that you've found the puncture.

6. Soft-leaded pencils.

7. A good eraser.

8. Pencils with erasers on the top.

9. Chocolate boxes.

10. The end credits and soothing music after the movie has finished.

11. Finding yourself holding two forks.

12. The sudden recognition that you are in good form today.

13. A woman who drives with panache.

14. Saying, "Saskatchewan".

15. The orchard smell in a room where an orange has been peeled.

16. Passing through a place that played a role in an old love affair and, irrationally, half-expecting to see the person you're thinking of.

17. Snow or rain at night that only comes into existence in the beam of a light.

18. When an acquaintance compliments
    you on your home-made pizza
    with the ridiculous suggestion
    that you could make a fortune if
    you opened your own pizzeria.

19. Two people sharing a plate of food.

20. A building that is transformed,
    because the name on it is that of a
    famous household product producer.

21. The joy of abiding by a piece of good
    advice and then seeing the benefits.

22. Sitting down comfortably with
    a cup of coffee and reading
    through the introduction
    manual of your new purchase.

23. The tuneless hum that people
    in a toilet make to indicate
    that they are there.

24. The wonderfully adult way of arranging an appointment, whereby you agree only to call beforehand if there's a problem.

25. Compact umbrellas that open at the press of a button.

26. The way a person scratches their head in an attempt to disguise the embarrassment of having waved unrequitedly at an acquaintance.

27. The exhuberant, collective whoop of a group of people running for shelter at the sudden onset of a downpour.

28. The sound of an inexperienced voice on a supermarket tannoy.

29. Old clothes that enable you to sit on the dusty ground.

30. Natural food packaging, like that of a banana, that you can simply throw over your shoulder when you've finished eating.

31. The fixed doll-like gaze of someone being kissed on the cheek.

32. What follows the expression:" Affectionately known as...".

33. The soft and affectionate manner that people adopt when speaking of their old primary school.

34. The way men look lovingly back at their cars as they walk away.

35. The novelty of hearing a song played backwards.

36. A mother and her young daughter standing together, and one looks just like a miniature version of the other.

37. The co-star in a TV series that becomes everyone's favourite.

38. The eternal optimism of opening the letterbox.

39. Impressive, yet meaningless statistics, like how many foot bridges there are in London.

40. Monocycles.

41. The magician's female assistant, who seems to do nothing more than stand, smile and hold her arms in the air.

42. Being the bearer of good news.

43. Bay windows.

44. Making a fair guess at where something might be, and then the pleasure of finding it there.

45. Gazing into the fridge for culinary inspiration.

46. Someone who smokes the occasional cigarette.

47. Photograghs of everyday objects from unusual angles that render them unrecognizable.

48. The last remaining pile of snow after the thaw.

49. When pouring from a jug:
    increasing the distance between
    it and the receptacle, and
    creating a long elastic line.

50. The "dance" that people
    do when talking agitatedly
    into a mobile phone.

51. Icicles.

52. The little, exciting game of trying
    to get into your house before
    your neighbour sees you.

53. Barbershop quartets.

54. Listening to someone's heartbeat.

55. Exotic fruit.

56. Putting your hand on something
    that has been warmed by the sun.

57. Coming across something in an
    unlikely place that would later have
    led to it being hopelessly lost.

58. Finding something you didn't
    realize you had lost.

59. When something you've been
    looking for for ages suddenly
    turns up unexpectedly.

60. A place you can only visit
    when the tide is out.

61. The good-natured pushing, shoving
    and mock outrage of two friends
    who are both insisting on paying.

62. Walking down the corridor of an old
    building and then, by means of an
    imperceptible connection, finding
    yourself in the new extension.

63. Waving back to someone
    who waved at you without
    knowing who they are.

64. Driving beside a train.

65. Splaying your fingers out
    after putting on gloves so
    that they fit snugly.

66. The rings of Saturn.

67. That slightly frustrating feeling you
    get when you see a car transporter
    with brand new models stacked
    on it as if they were worthless.

68. The child's ability to make
    the sweet last a long time.

69. How you can notice that a room
    has been cleaned by a woman.

70. A child whose pretence of
    being asleep is given away
    by the smile on its face.

71. When you've managed to nurse a
    bad experience into anecdote.

72. Remembering a past event so distant,
    that it feels like it never happened.

73. When someone you'd forgotten
    even existed somehow comes
    back into your memory.

74. People gallantly brushing their
    teeth before going to the dentist.

75. Holding a piece of tinted, transparent paper tightly to your face and seeing the world in a different colour.

76. The way children simply chant the name of something they want-often with great success.

77. The smell of old books.

78. When a person tilts their head back, winces, and looks up in a way which emphasizes that they are doing a quick mental calculation.

79. Arms folded in indignation.

80. Looking at the image of a beautiful woman on a billboard, while wondering who she really is and what she's doing at this very moment.

81. The joy of throwing a six.

82. The charming naivity of seeing
    a recent picture of a well-known
    actor and being shocked at
    how much they've aged.

83. A mannerism that is typical
    of a particular family.

84. Blossom trees.

85. Standing barefoot on a
    sun-warmed surface.

86. Stamping your shoes and
    giving them a good clean
    on a thick doormat.

87. Typewriters.

88. When you finally decide
    that something is not worth
    repairing anymore.

89. Looking out the window of
    an unfamiliar building and
    being surprised by which
    street you see outside.

90. That point in life when you begin
    to understand what people in
    those obscure jobs actually do.

91. The facade of a building
    that gives you no idea of
    where anything is inside.

92. Arches.

93. T-shirts with silly English
    words on them.

94. Rosary beads.

95. When the pizza baker throws
    the dough spinning in the air.

96. When someone stands up
    and they are much taller or
    smaller than you expected.

97. The effortless glamour of place
    names in the United States.

98. A small child kicking a football.

99. The glisten of spoked
    wheels in the sun.

100. The charming laziness of a household that still has the Christmas decorations up in the middle of February.

Gentil 3.

1. A good stretch in the morning.

2. Sandcastles.

3. Actually having postage stamps in the house.

4. Being up at an extremely early hour in a foreign country.

5. The stretched smile, bulging eyes and vigorous nodding of someone who wants to get away from a conversation.

6. Kids with hoarse voices.

7. Knowing the capitals of obscure countries.

8. When you think of all the mistakes and misdemeanours you've committed in your life that went unpunished.

9. An entrance, like that of a hotel, transformed by a canopy and a stretch of carpet.

10. The wheelspray from vehicles driving in heavy rain.

11. Pubs that have names appropriate to the area or the profession of their regulars.

12. Chess sets.

13. Autumn leaves.

14. Watching an uncoordinated person dancing vigorously.

15. The now seemingly incongruous working titles that famous films or songs once had.

16. A model of a car sitting in the back window of the real car.

17. A well-remembered theme to a favourite TV series or advertisement from your childhood.

18. Discovering new food.

19. A good joke that you can pass on for years.

20. When you can hear the next track on the album even before it has started.

21. Crumpling up a piece of paper, throwing it in the air, and then kicking it energetically like a football.

22. A really good mnemonic.

23. Domed roofs.

24. A child playing football and giving a running commentary at the same time.

25. At that stage of life where you define happiness as the absence of problems.

26. A song sung in English by someone who is clearly not a native speaker.

27. A friend pirouetting stiffly in front of you like a model, in order to display a new item of clothing that they are wearing.

28. When an acquaintance starts a conversation with, "Oh, I was talking to someone who knows you….".

29. A bespectacled person who looks totally different without their glasses.

30. When a guest, after having finished a coffee, takes the cup back to the kitchen to clean.

31. Being able to quickly decide not to do something because it's too much bother.

32. A photo of someone in mid-stride.

33. Railway junctions where the lines go off in all different directions.

34. The sound of an orchestra
    doing a last tune-up.

35. The wonderfully urban
    din of a screeching cat and
    a tumbling bin lid.

36. A drop of cold water on
    the back of your neck.

37. Answering questions that
    you like being asked.

38. Finally seeing the face behind
    a well-known radio voice.

39. Smokers in dressing gowns
    outside hospitals.

40. In barefeet trying to pick up
    something with your toes.

41. Throwing a bucket of water over a
    tiled surface before cleaning it.

42. Pages in a bible or old dictionary
    that have coloured edges.

43. Things that stack easily,
    like plates or chairs.

44. The smell of rain on a hot pavement.

45. Listening to a telephone
    conversation that consists only
    of, "Hmm-mm"and, "Yes".

46. Sunglasses on teddy bears.

47. Ivy-covered walls.

48. A house door that you have to knock.

49. When a person walking past
    the hairdressing salon seems to
    disappear, and then you realize
    that you were looking at a wall-
    mirror reflection of the street.

50. The secret wish to be able
    to wolf-whistle.

51. Jukeboxes.

52. Folding a piece of paper, then scissor-cutting some pieces out, so that when opened out again, it reveals a pattern.

53. The old-world feeling of someone richly whistling a tune.

54. When a truck with a crane on it is raised on metal stands for better stability and appears to be floating about a foot off the ground.

55. The new silence of the freshly oiled hinge.

56. Tiptoeing along.

57. When you pull on your trousers and then realize that your underpants from yesterday are still in them.

58. When you see an actor in a film playing a game or a musical instrument, and it's clear that they haven't a clue.

59. Thoughtfully chewing
    the top of a pencil.

60. A name that means nothing to you
    until you find out that this person
    invented something very important.

61. The names of racehorses.

62. Observatories.

63. Ice-cream vans.

64. A questionnaire that really
    makes you think about
    things you didn't before.

65. A funny expression or anecdote
    that your parents told you on
    countless occasions, and somehow
    you still managed to raise a smile.

66. When you discover that a short
    extract of music that you had
    always associated with a TV
    commercial is, in actual fact,
    from a famous classical piece.

67. Recognizing the footfall of
    someone you know well.

68. Those clever names they have
    for charity organizations.

69. When the phone rings
    unexpectedly and yet, somehow,
    you know who it is.

70. The resoundingly socialistic names
    of former communist institutions.

71. Roof gardens.

72. Two friends who look like each other.

73. Someone who strongly resembles
    their rock music hero.

74. African women carrying
    things on their heads.

75. When people's spectacles steam up.

76. The dog owner's unsuccessful
    attempt to command their pet.

77. Fixing a wobbly table by pushing
    a table mat under one of the legs.

78. Decorative floats made
for civic festivals.

79. Circus tents.

80. Waking up and then pleasantly
remembering that something you
painted yesterday will now be dry.

81. Rousing classical music that
you can't take seriously because
it's always used in circuses.

82. Barrel organs.

83. Countdowns.

84. Having to close your eyes while
being led to a surprise.

85. When a child puts its arms
akimbo and pouts.

86. The good-natured, mock
astonishment which adults
display when listening to a
child relating an incident.

87. Seeing a goal scored in a real football game and momentarily expecting the replay.

88. In the evening, watching a football game on TV that you already saw live that afternoon.

89. Grated cheese.

90. A car tyre round a lamppost.

91. Switching on the newly replaced light bulb.

92. Enthusiastic weather reporters.

93. Your favourite hairbrush.

94. A job requiring different tasks that can all be accomplished parallel to each other.

95. Humming a tune that is appropriate to the work you're doing.

96. Motorcades of football fans after a victory.

97. The enjoyment of indulging in a fallacy like the Loch Ness monster.

98. The sirens of foreign police cars and ambulances.

99. The amused astonishment of having just seen a mouse.

100. A birthday on a Saturday.

Gentil 4.

1. Ribbons.

2. Brass rubbings.

3. A nice piece of clothing that you only wear on special occasions.

4. The confectionery smell from a child's mouth.

5. Jumping over puddles.

6. Re-reading a book years later and being amazed at how much you've forgotten.

7. The slight sadness of a streetlamp on in the middle of the day.

8. The smell of a pencils.

9.   Picking up the last few words
     of a passerby's conversation
     and trying to work out what
     they were talking about.

10. People in the street in large
     furry animal costumes
     advertizing something.

11. Mosaics.

12. That strange instance when
     you are mentioning that you
     have lost something and, at
     that moment, you see it.

13. Hopscotch.

14. The squeals of children playing.

15. A boxer skipping.

16. A genuine compliment.

17. Cement mixers.

18. The way football referees adroitly
     jump over the ball when it
     comes to them during play.

19. Lollipops.

20. Lollipop sticks.

21. The word"Lollipop".

22. Looking up odd names in
    the telephone book.

23. The perforations that
    rain makes in sand.

24. Ships in bottles.

25. Things made of seashells.

26. Those strange little windowless
    houses with a warning on the
    door about high voltage.

27. Being in a shop that sells doors.

28. Someone carrying a large
    mirror down the street.

29. Strolling around a graveyard
    and reading the gravestones.

30. The changed perception of your home as you open the door after having been away for a while.

31. Wildlife films where the antelope gets away.

32. Getting a fine, high-pitched note from a wet glass by rubbing a finger around the rim.

33. When a tree has fallen into a lake and created a natural pier.

34. Famous criminal court cases.

35. Freshly painted road markings.

36. The shadow of a cloud moving across the landscape.

37. Disliking something that most other people seem to like and finally meeting someone who shares your view.

38. Children's finger graffiti on a grimy car.

39. A dog with a huge stick in its mouth.

40. Vehicles with caterpillar tracks.

41. Watching someone paste
    up a billboard poster.

42. An abacus.

43. People hugging each
    other at airports.

44. Grandfather clocks.

45. A lock of hair kept as a memento.

46. An endearing gesture of a loved one
    that you would never dare drawing
    attention to for fear that they would
    become self-conscious about it.

47. Your cut hairs on the
    hairdresser's floor.

48. An adult and a child on a motorbike.

49. A passenger plane flying
    low over traffic.

50. An airport where you actually drive under one of the runways.

51. How, regardless of how good or bad your memory is, you can instantly recognize a joke you've heard before.

52. The sudden breeze along the platform that tells you that the underground train is coming.

53. A kid's rucksack that looks like a cuddly toy.

54. The pun names that are given to drinks and meals in theme restaurants.

55. Guide dogs.

56. Gyroscopes.

57. Getting absolutely soaking wet and loving it.

58. When you squeeze a hot water bottle to expel the air, and a very particular rubbery aroma comes out.

59. The lifelong dialogue that
    goes on in a person's head.

60. How swearing has never really
    caught on in pop and rock songs.

61. The protective cover, similar to
    a lampshade, that the vet puts
    around a dog's head after surgery.

62. Bald barbers.

63. Four-poster beds.

64. Inflated job titles.

65. Goalkeepers.

66. Touching a part of your cheek
    and looking at someone to
    indicate where they have a
    piece of food on their face.

67. The first blast of heat when you get
    off the plane at a holiday destination.

68. A forgotten warning triangle on
    the hard shoulder of the road.

69. A small, religious shrine in
    an out-of-the-way place.

70. A child in whose face you can see
    the adult they will one day be.

71. A statistic, like the tonnage
    of a ship, which is both
    impressive and meaningless.

72. The white palms of an
    African's hands.

73. How different the grassy ground
    inside the tent seems.

74. Irrigation sprinklers.

75. An abandoned railway line.

76. When a road comes to a baffling end.

77. Great engineering follies.

78. Huge, road-making machines.

79. The tickly feeling when you pull
    out the shoelace that is trapped
    under the sole of your sock.

80. A door which has some sort of opening difficulty, which is known only to those familiar with it.

81. To be the first person to dive into the swimming pool.

82. The wobbly air above a heated surface.

83. The way men become enthusiastic cooks at a barbecue.

84. The smell of a barbecue.

85. A cement mixer hoisted up on a crane at the weekend, thus making it safe from theft.

86. When a couple of tourists reach their camera out to you and ask you to take a photo of them.

87. The rectangular space on a wall where a picture has been.

88. Starting a new address book.

89. Those huge microphones that Elvis used to sing into.

90. Ceilings with large beams.

91. A lamp, like that in a church, hung on a very long cord from a high ceiling.

92. Confessionals.

93. People who stick their tongue out when they're writing.

94. Scandinavians whose hair colour is lighter than their suntan.

95. Circular brickwork.

96. The sound of a cock crowing in the morning.

97. The posh sound of an expensive car's wheels on gravel.

98. The wide-eyed gaze of someone who's bored witless.

99. Freshly laid and rolled asphalt.

100. Goal-of-the-month competition.

Gentil 5.

1.   Thinking of a faraway, empty room.

2.   The smiling, rigid pose of the panting ice-skater after just finishing their performance.

3.   Towns on hills.

4.   Being the only passenger on a country bus.

5.   The large hanger on a hotel key.

6.   A festive hat in the back window of a car.

7.   Unpacking your suitcase after a holiday and finding that the clothes still retain the smell of the resort.

8. People who can put a candle
    out with their fingertips.

9. Seeing an object used for something
    it was never intended for.

10. Tree roots breaking
    through a pavement.

11. The urge to pour litres of water
    on a parched piece of ground.

12. Spoonerisms.

13. The child's love of cough medicine.

14. Kids' bathroom toys.

15. A word or name that you know
    well to see, but then are surprised
    when you first hear it pronounced.

16. Drum majors.

17. People who can adroitly spin a
    baton between their fingers.

18. When you discover that another person has a mutual animosity towards someone else which you then share together in a shower of recriminations.

19. The smell of ink markers.

20. Shaving brushes.

21. The mystery of why something unexpectedly falls over or collapses.

22. Women's underwear on a washing line.

23. The fresh, green trail between the long grass made by a mechanical lawn mower.

24. Those little man-size excavators that you see on building sites, and which are somehow hard to take seriously.

25. Holding a sheet of ice.

26. A one-room primary school.

27. People who lick their
    pencil before writing.

28. Someone clapping their hands
    and then rubbing them
    together in anticipation.

29. Enjoying making your teeth
    chatter even more in the cold.

30. The frozen smile of the passenger
    of a quickly passing car.

31. The smell of a hairdryer.

32. The excited, high-pitched
    voice of the athlete being
    interviewed just after the race.

33. Hearing a message at the airport
    requesting a Mr. Gonzales to go
    immediately to the information
    desk and wanting to go there as well
    to find out what the problem is.

34. Seaplanes.

35. Bare feet sinking into the wet sand.

36. The incorrect, albeit logical,
    way children spell things.

37. The spiral pattern of hair on
    the crown of a child's head that
    reminds you of the Milky Way.

38. A light in a window.

39. A fans' bus with pictures
    in the windows.

40. Looking down a stairwell and seeing
    a hand moving along the bannister.

41. When you ask some acquaintances
    if they know a particular song
    and they reply by bursting into a
    loud and tuneless rendition of it.

42. Mud-covered rugby players.

43. Kitschy religious souvenirs.

44. Hieroglyphics.

45. People who can read heiroglyphics.

46. Elaborate models made of
    thousands of matchsticks.

47. When looking at the foundation markings of a house noticing how small it seems.

48. Nice streetlamps.

49. The ingenious, compact, storage spaces in caravans and boats.

50. When a woman with long hair tied up in a bun lets it down in flowing adundance.

51. The round stain left by a wet glass that cleans off easily.

52. Polishing an apple shiny before biting into it.

53. The sound of tyres on a wet street.

54. Joggers prancing on the spot at the traffic lights.

55. Old delivery bikes with a small wheel and rack at the front.

56. The sound of crickets.

57. The fact that you can't
    see the crickets.

58. The amazing sequence of swearwords
    that comes out of a person's
    mouth when they stub their toe.

59. The tendency, especially
    among children, to close
    their eyes while hiding.

60. Running your hand along the prickly
    hairs on the back of your neck just
    after having been to the hairdresser's.

61. Asking a couple how they met.

62. Police officers eating an ice cream.

63. A row of footballers
    holding their genitals.

64. Tree houses.

65. Garments with a spare button
    considerately attached.

66. Catching up on the news
    after having been away.

67. Watching the players of the national football team unsuccessfully trying to sing the national anthem.

68. The nicknames of old units of currency.

69. Dimples.

70. Cossack dancers who squat and then kick out their legs alternately.

71. Floodlit football games where the players seem to have four shadows.

72. Copper rooftops on institutional buildings that go green with time.

73. Clipping your toenails which are nice and soft after the bath.

74. A Harlem church service where everyone is clapping and singing.

75. A dog chasing a stick.

76. Running your hand over a completed jigsaw.

77. Walking up a set of stairs, then further on walking down a similar set, because you're in a building that was originally two separate houses.

78. Someone you don't know but recognize as the brother or sister of someone you do know.

79. A bicycle with a very high-positioned seat, obviously for a very tall person.

80. An ant carrying a leaf.

81. Remembering the name of a pen friend.

82. Megaphones.

83. Photographic yearbooks.

84. Poster shops.

85. The ascending "cluck-cluck" sound of a bottle being filled.

86. A freshly hosed-down pavement.

87. Swiss army knives.

88.   Tracing paper.

89.   Balsa wood.

90.   The charcoal stripes on grilled food.

91.   Lookalike contests.

92.   The name of a local bus or train
      destination that you know well
      but have never been to.

93.   Famous sunken ships.

94.   Shoals of fish.

95.   Turning the dial on a radio tuner
      and listening to the different
      stations fading in and out.

96.   Sumo wrestlers.

97.   Paper aeroplanes.

98.   Those old French cars where the
      door hinges are behind the passenger
      and so the door opens to the front.

99.   City marathons.

100. A lost scarf or glove hung on
a branch, so that the searcher
can find it more easily.

Gentil 6.

1.   A name written large
on a sandy beach.

2.   When a row of cars turns into a
sunlit street and one by one the
drivers pull their sunshades down.

3.   Fingerprints.

4.   The affection you feel for astronauts.

5.   Chestnuts.

6.   Collecting chestnuts.

7. When a chestnut suddenly
    falls to the ground.

8. Small railway vehicles worked
    by a handle pumped up and
    down by one or two people.

9. The huge, mechanical parts of a mill.

10. When a child learns to whistle.

11. The nicknames schoolkids
    give their teachers.

12. The way foreign waiters, no
    matter how long they've been in
    the country, still count up the
    bill in their native tongue.

13. Limericks.

14. Pigtails.

15. Butter melting in the hot pan.

16. When an acquaintance ignores your
    greeting and rushes past you, because
    they are dying to go to the toilet.

17. Firemen sliding down a pole.

18. A hat blowing off in the wind.

19. Postponing opening an important
    letter until the evening, so as
    not to risk ruining your day.

20. When the doorbell rings and
    several people answer the intercom
    system and end up talking
    confusedly to each other.

21. A horse asleep standing.

22. Stirring your tea or coffee really
    fast and then watching the
    surface spinning around.

23. Jamaican steel bands.

24. The wonderful mental arithmetic
    of the darts player.

25. Printers' boxes.

26. The distant roar from the
    football ground telling you
    that a goal has just gone in.

27. The names of different
    punctuation marks.

28. The sudden, not-unpleasant
    feeling in your stomach that
    tells you that you're hungry.

29. Lipstick.

30. Your dentist chatting away amicably
    to you, but you can only nod back
    and grunt because your mouth is full
    cotton wool and dental instuments.

31. Someone on a bicycle with one
    hand on another bicycle that they
    are transporting for some reason.

32. Children's books or cards
    that fold out to create a
    three-dimensional form.

33. A large hole in the street, dug
    as part of some maintenance
    work, that gives you a view
    into the underground world of
    drainage and sewage pipes that
    you would normally never see.

34. When an old enemy is
    down on his luck.

35. The old-world sight of people picking
    berries from roadside bushes.

36. The shapes and colours of
    rooftops in different countries.

37. In a cosmetics shop spraying
    on a sample of the perfume
    that your loved one uses.

38. The lost glove on the pathway.

39. Quoting a proverb that compliments
    the person you're talking to.

40. A dry, rectangular patch on
    a wet street where a recently
    parked car has been.

41. The file search facility on your PC where the numbers and letters change so fast that it looks like some sort of squiggly animation.

42. Those little wire things that cut a boiled egg into neat slices.

43. Getting up early when you don't have to.

44. At the change of every month how people say, "My God, where has the year gone?"

45. Catholic church masses where half the congregation don't know when to stand up or sit down.

46. Short cuts.

47. A foreigner speaking an unintelligible language but which is punctuated with words of local reference that are in your language.

48. An ancient, worn-out wallet
    like the one that contains your
    driving licence that you would
    never even think of changing.

49. Stamps that you don't have to lick.

50. Female speed skaters.

51. Female speed skaters' thighs.

52. Female speed skaters pulling off their
    cap triumphantly at the end of the
    race and letting their hair flow out.

53. A bird having a bath.

54. Braille.

55. Eating food that is in season.

56. Shoeboxes.

57. Accidentally kicking a stone
    and it travels much further
    than you expected.

58. Women who smile and
    wink with both eyes.

59. When the wind whistles.

60. A walk along a beach on a windy day.

61. A piece of graffiti in a place that seems almost inaccessible.

62. A row of bicycles falling over domino style.

63. Rope ladders.

64. When someone in the street speaks to their partner in an extremely rude way, and then you realize that they are talking to the dog that's with them.

65. The names of flowers.

66. Accordians.

67. A tree-lined road.

68. Taking a nap in the sun.

69. The smell of new books.

70. Adding more hot water to the bath you're in.

71. The smell of a flowerbed.

72. Aquarium screensavers.

73. Getting distracted while looking up a word in a dictionary and spending the following fifteen minutes looking at other words.

74. In the middle of a conversation with a friend trying to retrace the topics to find out how you arrived at the present one.

75. An unopened lucky dip.

76. To stay in your car in the car wash.

77. People who are just big kids, really.

78. Sayings that are paradoxical.

79. When your anti-virus program asks you if you want to delete the found virus and you joyfully slap the "OK" button.

80. Someone pointedly telling another passenger on the bus to lift their bag off the seat they want to sit on.

81. A car transporting a piece of furniture on the roof.

82. Seeing a sofa attached to the roof of a car and imagining what fun it would be to be sitting on it.

83. The people who look after the animals at the zoo.

84. Penguins just standing around.

85. When a cat crouches.

86. When you momentarily take someone else's supermarket trolley.

87. The mechanical, yet cheery, voice of the next stop announcing machine on the tram.

88. The children's game of lying on the floor and pressing the soles of your feet against those of another.

89. Acappella singing.

90. The rhythmic sound of the train's wheels going over the sleepers.

91. A child that you can see is only a few years away from becoming a beautiful adult.

92. A photo of a UFO taken in the 1950's that looks like a 1950's UFO.

93. When the weightlifter falls over backwards.

94. Lying on the sand and letting the tide creep up your legs.

95 The fluttering shadow of a leafy branch on a wall.

96. Chimney sweeps.

97. When a foreigner learning your language uses an endearing colloquialism.

98. A woman rubbing her hands with moisturizing cream.

99. Playfully splashing water at someone.

100. Biting the bottom of an ice-cream cone off and then sucking the remainder of the ice cream out.

Gentil 7.

1.   Torches.

2.   The sound of horses' hooves.

3.   Suddenly realizing that you're
      singing a song that you hate.

4.   Film trailers.

5.   Looking for the light switch on
      a part of the wall where it had
      been in a previous home.

6.   The way people hold themselves up
      straight and smile for a photo.

7.   Closing a low drawer with your foot.

8.   The fierce smile of someone showing
      you their new dental work.

9. The front seat at the top of
    a double-decker bus.

10. The names people give their cats.

11. Snow on rooftops.

12. A candlelit bathroom.

13. Pine forests.

14. Hitting the light switch so
    quickly that you turn it off
    again and then find yourself
    walking into a darkened room.

15. When the train goes around
    a long bend and you can
    see the other carriages.

16. Birds landing on water.

17. Shire horses.

18. Wooden jigsaws.

19. The sound of seagulls.

20. A brightly painted, cut-away
    model of a machine.

21. The moving shadows on a wall, caused by the headlights of a passing car.

22. L-shaped sofas.

23. Cycling on a warm night

24. Standing on a bridge going over a motorway.

25. Enjoying munching on a meal while you're still cooking it.

26. Managing to stay seated on your bicycle by holding onto the post at the traffic lights.

27. Someone running after their hat on a windy day.

28. Pleasantly realizing that you have forgotten and missed an appointment that you didn't want to go to anyway.

29. The names of different Italian noodles.

30. Using a friend's back as a
    leaning board to write on.

31. The spray from a fountain.

32. A very old person smiling
    affectionately at a young couple.

33. Seeing another motorist swaying
    their head and singing.

34. Magnets.

35. Long shadows on sunny
    autumn days.

36. As a customer:to find yourself
    behind the counter for some reason.

37. The gentle clink of a spoon
    stirring in a cup.

38. The unsuccessful attempt to cover
    up the price tag on a present.

39. Seeing a familiar street from
    an unfamiliar angle.

40. The way we finish eating a meal
    so that there is still one element of
    each foodstuff on the last forkful.

41. The dramatic part of a kids' film
    at the cinema, when the children
    shout out warnings to the hero.

42. Waving your hands in front of
    the TV so that it appears that
    you have twenty fingers.

43. Making shadows on the
    wall with your fingers.

44. The day you reach a certain
    age that you remember your
    parents once being.

45. Words that are pronounced
    differently from how they are spelt.

46. Scissors that are so sharp, that all
    you have to do is run the open
    blades through the paper.

47. When the taxi driver takes you home by a different, but just as efficient, route.

48. Foreign money.

49. The slightly different feeling to your car or bicycle after it has been repaired.

50. Making a tent out of a bed blanket.

51. Watching a good card player shuffle cards.

52. Snowflakes under a microscope.

53. When the camera remains focussed on the newsreader after he has finished.

54. Magnifying glasses.

55. Jumping back into bed.

56. The holiday smell of sweat and suntan lotion.

57. Regional accents.

58. Cheese slices that are exactly the same size as the bread.

59. The relief of waking up from a bad dream.

60. Sitting in the shade of a tree on a hot day.

61. The smell of new clothes.

62. The indented line on a woman's hair, indicating where a hairband or the rim of a hat had been.

63. Fans.

64. Oddly shaped cases designed to accommodate musical instruments or technical equipment.

65. Freshly ironed clothes piled neatly on a shelf.

66. Summer dresses.

67. Drinking cold water on a hot day and feeling it going all the way down to your stomach.

68. The thick bicycle lock around someone's neck that makes them look like a lord mayor.

69. The double stick attached to newspapers in cafes to prevent theft.

70. Bales of hay.

71. The sort of suitcase that you only see in movies:beautifully packed with neat bundles of bank notes.

72. When you drop something made of glass and, miraculously, it doesn't break.

73. Actors acting eating.

74. Talking about what you would do if you had a lot of money.

75. A good dog showing divine patience while being hauled about by kids.

76. When a friend leaves something behind at your place.

77. Gift wrapping.

78. Bringing your bicycle to a halt
    and then balancing on the
    pedals for as long as possible.

79. The last half-dozen
    pieces of the jigsaw.

80. Sun showers.

81. Water fountains.

82. When the wind blows the leaves on
    the ground into a miniature tornado.

83. Clocks that chime.

84. Old vending machines.

85. The names of the different general
    secretaries of the United Nations.

86. Tail fin designs on airliners.

87. Morning dew.

88. An open cliff face where you can
    see the different layers of rock.

89. The unwritten pact between people whereby they never reveal the ending of a book or film.

90. Looking in the mirror to check your appearance and then hearing a totally unconnected burst of laughter from outside.

91. The sudden surprise when putting an object down and at the same time a loud noise occurs somewhere else.

92. A landscape at night suddenly illuminated by a flash of lightning.

93. The sick, husky voice that people adopt when relating a previous illness, or when phoning in ill.

94. Shots of film extras off-set having a chat and a cigarette while a large spear is sticking out of their backs.

95. The little hop that ballet dancers and acrobats do when coming on or leaving the stage.

96. The ink drawings and lettering that kids do on their schoolbags.

97. The open-door light from a fridge in a darkened kitchen.

98. The dissolving colours on a soap bubble just before it bursts.

99. Football grounds where you can see houses in the background.

100. Putting on a shirt that's still warm from the radiator.

Gentil 8.

1. When someone returns a borrowed
   item in an improved condition.

2. Singing at the top of your voice
   while underway in your car.

3. When someone calls to cancel
   an appointment that you didn't
   want to go to anyway.

4. Looking at the menu in
   a box of chocolates.

5. The beeping of a truck that
   sounds like a ship's horn.

6. When the doctor taps you
   on different parts of your
   body with his fingers.

7. Reading on the toilet.

8. Ashtrays with a spinning disc
    activated by a button with
    the palm of your hand.

9. The bowl-shaped slab on the shop
    counter for lifting your change off.

10. The snoring sound made
    by the coffee maker.

11. Thermos flasks.

12. The type of cold that gives you
    a thunderous, bass voice.

13. The hum of several machines
    in the kitchen running
    simultaneously, giving you a
    strong feeling of industriousness.

14. The cosiness of the car-interior light.

15. The person who's in a film because
    they are a celebrity in some other
    area and whose inability to act
    sticks out like a sore thumb.

16. A woman performing the seemingly impossible act of taking off her bra while leaving her pullover on.

17. A person who speaks perfect English but with a combination of accents that makes it impossible to place.

18. Striped toothpaste.

19. A long train transporting cars, that at first looks like some sort of comic-book traffic jam.

20. The mesmerized gaze of a child watching a cartoon on TV.

21. Changing the position of your bed.

22. When a person takes a sharp intake of breath pre-empting an important statement.

23. How the enjoyment of an experience is enhanced when shared with a friend.

24. Cutting a pile of freshly made sandwiches into neat triangles.

25. The dark, crustier side
    of a slice of bread.

26. American fire trucks.

27. Calmly pressing tightly on
    something that deflates slowly,
    like a dinghy or swim ring.

28. A word written in letters
    that are appropriate to the
    meaning of the word.

29. An articulated lorry travelling
    at speed without its trailer.

30. Singing in the bath.

31. When singing in the bath
    reaching a pitch that seems
    to resound more loudly.

32. Men working on a roof.

33. Listening to the traffic news about
    traffic jams that you are not in.

34. When you take the same evasive manoeuvres as an oncoming pedestrian and end up apologetically bumping into each other.

35. People, with little wheels on a metal shaft, measuring the road.

36. When the boss is away for a few days.

37. Yodelling.

38. Hearing an acquaintance sing for the first time.

39. The handball goalkeeper's in-vain dance before the penalty shot goes rocketing past him.

40. Looking through a professional journal that you know nothing about.

41. Reading a local paper from an area you don't know.

42. The relief of finding out that the sudden plop on your head was a drop of water and not from a bird.

43. The day after washing your
    hair and it's nicely pressed
    down from sleeping.

44. Metal measuring tape that
    spins back into the container
    when you press a button.

45. A shop sign with a letter missing.

46. A car number plate that
    spells something odd.

47. Wondering where jokes come from.

48. One-hit wonders.

49. An old person singing an
    old song in an old voice.

50. An old village pump.

51. Blond hair and dark eyebrows.

52. A perfectly clean blackboard.

53. Writing with chalk.

54. Books by the same author that have a continual, and instantly recognizable, cover design.

55. When dolphins jump briefly out of the water.

56. The extra hour's sleep you get when the clocks go back.

57. Tracing paper.

58. Kilts.

59. Speculating about what is worn under the kilt.

60. Cheerful postmen.

61. A tall acquaintance who looks even taller every time you see them.

62. Lying in bed on a day off and musing that at this time you would already have been at work for two hours.

63. The big hat that a chef wears.

64. Footballers' names that sound like footballers' names.

65. Groups of Eastern European men who all shake hands with each other.

66. Eastern European men who kiss each other three times on the cheeks.

67. When the assistants in a shop serving an elderly person refer to them as "young lady"or "young man".

68. When an official asking for your signature refers to it as your autograph.

69. A ketchup bottle that's been washed transparently clean.

70. Taking visitors around your home town and rediscovering the beauty and interest of it for yourself.

71. Blotters.

72. A person wearing a sandwich board.

73. The television in the DIY shop showing a short film on how to use some sort of wallpaper paste that is mesmerizing in its boredom.

74. Someone giving you a lift.

75. The chattiness of the person you are giving a lift to.

76. A photographer focussing on something with his camera on a sunny autumn day.

77. A person using an extra bit of free time to tidy up the data on their mobile phone.

78. Going into the next room to get something and then coming back with something else.

79. Unfinished works by great artists.

80. That hard-to-place whining noise of air escaping from the slightly opened top of a fizzy drink bottle.

81. The lovely, silly little names of IKEA products.

82. Blinking lights at roadworks which flash but don't dazzle you.

83. Radar stations.

84. Putting your cold hands round a warm cup of something.

85. A person whom you always regard as older than you, but who isn't.

86. Miniature railways.

87. Rubbing the silver foil on a chocolate bar and seeing a relief pattern underneath.

88. Cylindrical pillows.

89. Liquorice.

90. Sawdust.

91. A basement window from where you can only see people's feet going by.

92. Sewing boxes.

93. An oven door with a window.

94. Speeded-up film of a flower opening, or a cake baking.

95. The nowadays seldom courtesy
    of someone taking off their
    hat when entering a room
    or talking to someone.

96. Using your feet to push
    off your shoes.

97. Slip-on shoes that you
    can just step out of.

98. The view of a coastline from
    a plane where you can see the
    land underneath the sea.

99. People, usually young, who pull
    faces behind someone being
    interviewed outside on television.

100. When you tell someone that you
     have lost something and they
     respond by helpfully, but illogically,
     looking around their own feet.

Gentil 9.

1. A piece of an iceberg falling off
   and crashing into the sea.

2. The banal, and obviously reluctant,
   little speech that the pilot makes
   over the intercom to the passengers.

3. The wake of a speeding
   boat seen from the air.

4. Sea horses.

5. A shooting star

6. A small, regional hotel
   with flags from all over the
   world flying outside.

7. Crispy, frosted grass in
   the early morning.

8. When you're thinking of something really funny, but are in a situation where you shouldn't laugh.

9. A bird sitting on a hippo's head.

10. Seeing the firemen in the speeding fire engine still getting dressed.

11. The high-pitched, husky voice of someone yawning and talking at the same time.

12. When the label peels off really easily.

13. The names of patron saints of unusual things.

14. A ploughed field.

15. A harmless snowball fight.

16. How people turn when they're putting on a shoulder bag.

17. Wet tracks coming out of a puddle.

18. Putting on something you haven't worn for a long time.

19. Tidying up your desk instead
of getting on with the work.

20. Having the courage to throw an
unopened letter into the rubbish bin.

21. The swish of a girl's ponytail
when she's jogging.

22. Shaking the fused bulb
beside your ear.

23. On an evening out with
someone and, when ordering,
they announce that they will
have whatever you're having.

24. The top bunk bed.

25. Tuning forks.

26. On seeing a new piece of graffiti, the
mystery of who did it and when.

27. A half-demolished building where
you can see the room interiors.

28. A person with a strange accent.

29. Those little creatures that
    only live for a day.

30. Talking to the hairdresser
    in the mirror.

31. Billboard posters that have been
    pasted on askew, making the
    people depicted look deformed.

32. Hearing a strange noise from your
    neighbour's place and trying to
    work out what they're doing.

33. How the eyes of a passenger on a
    train flick from side to side as the
    person gazes out the window.

34. When you watch something fall, and
    it seems like slow motion, and you
    are so entranced that you don't react.

35. Drawing a map of the
    area where you live.

36. A make-up or paint catalogue with
    little squares of different colours.

37. Bird tracks in the snow.

38. Whistling key rings(whatever happened to them?).

39. The way someone, when talking agitatedly on the phone, starts to superficially tidy their desk.

40. A truck carrying just the cabin section of another truck which is mounted in a backwards position and so, at first glance, gives the impression that it is travelling in reverse at an astonishing speed.

41. A heavy object that is neither locked nor secured, because it is simply too heavy to steal.

42. The way polystyrene seems to heat up in your hand.

43. When the pop group on TV keeps on moving and miming after the music has faded out.

44. A photo of someone in mid-air.

45. The imprint of letters on a book
cover, which had been used at some
earlier time as something to lean on.

46. Two people each taking off a glove
so that they can hold hands.

47. Listening to the sound of
the sea in a seashell.

48. The scribbling on a page
indicating where someone
had tried out a biro pen.

49. A curtain slowly moving in
the heat above a radiator.

50. Someone laughing while
they're lying down.

51. When your head or hand is
on someone's chest and you
can feel the resonance of their
voice through their rib cage.

52. People who move their lips
when they are reading.

53. When you feel your hands warming up again.

54. A street that has the same name as one you used to live in.

55. Velcro.

56. Toys in a cereal packet.

57. Someone still holding their open umbrella long after it has stopped raining.

58. The small, illuminated glass case outside the restaurant with the menu and prices in it.

59. When you suddenly remember that the muscle pains you have are from an intensive session of lovemaking the previous day.

60. Eavesdropping in on a guided tour of a museum.

61. A long, but leisurely, stroll to someone you want to visit.

62. Answering the phone and then holding the receiver close to the stereo, so that your caller can hear some of the lovely music you're listening to.

63. The theatrical semaphore of two people giving and receiving directions.

64. The way you can simply tell that someone is walking to their car and not out for a stroll.

65. People who sing enthusiastically through the chorus of a song, but then sit looking baffled during the rest of it.

66. Oil patterns in water.

67. Finding, and examining, someone else's shopping list in the trolley.

68. The incredible grimace that some people pull when they are singing-or at least trying to.

69. Seeing a really famous actor in a very small part in a film made much earlier in their career.

70. The light, pleasurable feeling you get when finding out from some biographical details that the person lived a very long time.

71. People who can predict the weather by just looking at the sky.

72. A pencil sharpened at both ends.

73. A tired person raising a smile.

74. The slowly fading power light on a machine that has just been switched off.

75. A message left on your answering machine by someone who had not thought about what they wanted to say.

76. Having to park somewhere
    totally illegal, and then coming
    back hours later to find that
    you got away with it.

77. The little standing walk
    that a woman does when
    hitching up her jeans.

78. The fine, discreet graphics on
    the package of medicine for
    an embarrassing problem.

79. A woman standing in a racing-
    leg position, with a shoulder bag
    balanced on her front thigh that
    she is rummaging through.

80. Accidentally making a pun.

81. Hearing an interesting
    discussion on the car radio.

82. Turning the steering wheel
    with the palm of your hand.

83. The sweet, perfumed after-smell from
    two old ladies who have just gone by.

84. When you realize that the motorcyclist is female.

85. A brief beep of a car horn indicating that someone is saying hello to you.

86. Old metal cigarette cases.

87. A bird flying a few metres in front of you while you're driving or cycling.

88. A hand reaching out of a car sunroof to wave goodbye.

89. Watching someone fold a T-shirt correctly.

90. The clever manoeuvring you do in order to avoid getting into a conversation with someone.

91. Icebreakers.

92. The little "dunk" sound a florescent light makes when it comes on.

93. A task that you don't really want to do, but which gives you an excuse not to do another, less pleasant, task.

94. A parent returning home from the primary school on a kid's bike.

95. Two schoolboys exchanging football cards.

96. The invisible parking space that most people don't see.

97. The crestfallen look on a person's face when they discover that there is a long queue.

98. Someone calling you to come into the living room quickly because there's something really funny on TV.

99. Those actors who always play the villain.

100. When things get so bad that you just have to sit down and laugh.

Gentil 10.

1. The light of a full moon that
    makes everything look like it's
    covered in a fine, white dust.

2. When, after moving furniture
    around, a particular piece finds
    a new-and better-position.

3. Finding things down the
    back of the sofa.

4. The way a person waves their hand,
    indicating that they need a pen.

5. A novel that starts with a map.

6. Light flooding into a room
    when you draw the curtains.

7. Footprint patterns of shoes.

8. The happy-go-lucky posing in
   pictures of pop groups from the 60's.

9. Walking barefoot on wet grass.

10. A freshly mopped floor.

11. The images created in your
    head by the names of the
    great rivers of the world.

12. Actually seeing the bird in the
    tree that's making the song.

13. Large, mechanical cranes.

14. Those seemingly never-ending goods
    trains rolling over the level crossing.

15. Bamboo.

16. People raising their umbrellas
    as they pass each other.

17. The smell that houses in
    other countries have.

18. The"faces" that different cars have.

19. Children's coloured chalkmarks on the pavement.

20. The smell of woodsmoke.

21. Combine harvesters.

22. Car keys.

23. Rubbing a herb like basil in your fingers and then smelling it.

24. Eating a little bit of the fresh parsley you've just bought.

25. A thick, silky bracelet on a woman's arm, that is actually a hairband.

26. Looking into the front window of a house and seeing right through to the back window and the garden beyond.

27. Sitting on a high table and swinging the below-the-knee parts of your legs to and fro.

28. Vases.

29. The royal suits in a pack of cards.

30. Metronomes.

31. Watching someone concentrate.

32. Opening ceremonies for great events.

33. National anthems that sound
    like the background music
    to an old comedy film.

34. Groups of nuns on an outing.

35. The names of heavy metal bands.

36. Spinning tops.

37. The boisterous whoops of two young
    people on a bicycle made for one.

38. The Latin or Greek names
    for geometric shapes.

39. Waterfalls.

40. The smell of freshly washed clothes.

41. The names of holiday or weekend
    houses in other languages.

42. Birds sitting on a wire or ledge.

43. A dog sticking its nose out of the window of a moving car and enjoying the headwind.

44. Browsing in a bookshop.

45. Discovering a new author all on your own.

46. The away strip of a football team that makes them look totally different.

47. Helicopters.

48. The photo of a street you know well taken fifty years ago.

49. A woman putting on make-up.

50. A couple kissing in the street.

51. Padlocks.

52. Voice impersonators.

53. Cobblestone surfaces.

54. Large church bells.

55. Spiral staircases.

56. Elaborate lettering on
    a shop window.

57. Watching a sheepdog in action.

58. When the TV presenter talks
    to the wrong camera.

59. Denim.

60. Clear, plastic covers for documents.

61. The mistakes in films.

62. LP cover designs from the sixties.

63. Children talking in a
    foreign language.

64. Tai Chi.

65. Driving down a local road that
    you've never been down before.

66. Coming over the crest of a hill.

67. Catamarans.

68. A person helping another person
    to park by holding out their arms,
    and then closing them slowly to
    show the driver how much space
    they still have, usually ending with
    a raised hand and a brisk shout.

69. The very convincing, imitation,
    light plastic TVs, stereos and
    monitor screens used for display
    purposes in furniture stores.

70. The existence of tiny countries
    like Andorra and Liechtenstein.

71. Lying with your eyes closed, then
    feeling the increasing temperature
    and brightness on your eyelids
    as the sun comes out.

72. The funny, wonky sound a
    pot with swirling water in it
    makes when you accidentally
    bump it against something.

73. Seeing someone in a park on a
    sunny day lying and reading.

74. Sign language.

75. A child chasing birds.

76. Carousels.

77. The sound of shutters being drawn up in the morning.

78. Boating lakes.

79. Seeing the film of the book.

80. Kites.

81. The joy of getting cleaned up after a long and sticky journey.

82. Kids holding their noses and jumping from the high board in a swimming pool.

83. Owls.

84. While watching a TV film successfully remembering where you had seen the actor before.

85. Seeing a toy red balloon high in the sky floating away.

86. Pencil cases.

87. Vapour trails.

88. To look at a crescent moon in a blue, daylight sky and, with a little concentration, perceive it as a sphere.

89. The sound of ice cubes in a drink.

90. Cycling with the wind at your back.

91. Watching small children eat.

92. When you start to read an old magazine instead of throwing it out.

93. Seeing the traffic jam on the other side of the motorway.

94. The rainbow colours on the play side of a CD.

95. The convex reflection of a room in a silver ball.

96. Drawing a circle with a compass.

97. The feeling after the first beer.

98. The changing expression on
    people's faces as they watch
    TV, or a film at the cinema.

99. Public posters, on which crossed eyes
    and missing teeth have been drawn.

100. Peeling a warm, hard-boiled egg
     under cold running water.

Gentil 11.

1. The smell of sun-grown tomatoes.

2. Turning the pillow over to the cold side at night.

3. The silent slurping of kids eating ice cream.

4. Someone running-and catching-a bus.

5. Waking up after a siesta.

6. Suddenly remembering why you came into the kitchen.

7. Going downhill on a bicycle.

8. The feeling when the train finally departs.

9. Closing your eyes and raising
    your face to the sun.

10. Waking up with a start, then
    realizing that it's Sunday morning.

11. Washing your hair under the shower.

12. The feeling in your stomach when
    the first coffee of the day takes effect.

13. Receiving a brightly
    coloured airmail letter.

14. Pressing the button and the lift
    doors open immediately.

15. Getting a window seat.

16. Finding a packet of chewing
    gum and some money in
    an old jacket pocket.

17. Talking to a nice old person.

18. A long-awaited pee.

19. Changing into looser clothing
    after coming home.

20. Birds singing in the early morning.

21. Blowing bubbles.

22. A good sneeze.

23. Putting on perfume.

24. Pulling funny faces in the bathroom mirror.

25. Lying on the ground.

26. Looking up at the sky and pretending that it's below you.

27. The smell of freshly cut grass.

28. Drinking some water in the middle of the night.

29. A dream about someone you hardly know.

30. Flicking through the pages of a new book.

31. Watering a plant.

32. Throwing a piece of clothing across a room and into a laundry basket.

33. People yawning after each other.

34. Hearing someone laugh.

35. The sound of someone
    playing the piano.

36. Looking up at the rain at night.

37. Someone running and
    smiling at the same time.

38. Finding your keys.

39. Seeing faces and giants in the clouds.

40. Polishing shoes.

41. Putting on glasses to read something.

42 Putting on heeled shoes
    and feeling taller.

43. Someone calling your name.

44. Drawing faces on a steamy window.

45. Hot water evaporating off
    a freshly boiled egg.

46. Watching someone tying
    their shoelaces.

47. The sudden surprise of hailstones.

48. After the dental check-up.

49. A freshly cleaned car interior.

50. The sound of rain on a tent roof.

51. The smell of ironing.

52. Slowly immersing in a hot bath.

53. Vacuum cleaning a sandy carpet.

54. A parking space right out front.

55. Coming out of the cinema
    after a good film.

56. Reading obituaries of famous
    people you've never heard of.

57. Reflections of streetlights
    on a wet street.

58. Walking in the snow.

59. The blinking light on your
    answering machine.

60. Nosing around someone else's house.

61. Wrapping up in a lovely warm towel.

62. When the train comes
    out of the tunnel.

63. Running your hand across
    a flat stomach.

64. The silence of three o'clock
    in the morning.

65. Kids watching workmen
    down a hole.

66. Hearing advertisement
    jingles in Danish.

67. Seeing the newsreader talk about
    problems in Middle America,
    while behind him there is a
    picture of Kermit the frog.

68. Hearing someone who
    can't sing, sing.

69. Throwing stones into water.

70. Peeing while having a bath.

71. Rainbows.

72. Rain falling so hard, that it
    looks as if there are thousands
    of little ducks in the street.

73. Hot-water bottles.

74. Opening an envelope
    with a sharp knife.

75. The secret doors in
    castles and palaces.

76. Trying to remember the people
    in an old address book.

77. Someone scratching your itch.

78. Old film of early attempts to fly.

79. Magnifying glasses.

80. Putting the letter into the envelope.

81. Black sprinters.

82. Walking barefoot in the sand.

83. Finding your unfinished coffee.

84. When the plane rises
    above the clouds.

85. Old science fiction movies.

86. Jumping into the water.

87. Tabloid headlines.

88. After-the-rain smell.

89. Being naked in an empty house.

90. Sunshine blinking through the
    trees while you're driving.

91. An armchair with a footrest.

92. While driving, seeing trees
    appear out of the mist.

93. The round, transparent holes
    in steamed-up bus windows
    that people have made.

94. Discovering new music.

95. Writing with a thick pen.

96. Using a garden hose.

97. Birds flying in formation.

98. Writing on a blank page.

99. Ripples on water.

100. New soap.

Gentil 12.

1. Looking into a fire.

2. Kicking leaves.

3. When your favourite part
   in a song comes.

4. Someone turning on the light
   in a room and then you realize
   how dark it had been.

5. A gust of wind.

6. The reflection of a complete
   landscape in a lake.

7. A spider's web with water droplets.

8. Driving through a tunnel
   with the windows down.

9. Poking a hole in the vacuum
   seal of a coffee jar.

10. Momentarily putting the
    wrong lid on something.

11. Lifting something that was much
    lighter than you thought .

12. A window dummy suddenly moving,
    because it's really a shop employee.

13. Architectural models.

14. Noticing for the first time
    that your dustpan is actually
    quite a nice shape.

15. Watching an informal game of
    soccer on a Sunday afternoon.

16. Looking up and suddenly
    seeing the moon.

17. Driving licence photos.

18. Tossing a pancake in a pan.

19. Hot-air balloons.

20. Kittens.

21. Someone nice touching your
    arm when talking to you.

22. The purring of a cat.

23. Music that makes you cry.

24. The sound and touch of falling snow.

25. Birds circling in the air.

26. The names of hurricanes
    and typhoons.

27. New coloured pencils.

28. The memories that a
    particular song brings.

29. Thick socks.

30. Public clocks that also tell
    you the temperature.

31. Momentarily meeting a
    stranger's glance, and they
    respond by smiling at you.

32. How early-morning people
    greet each other.

33. Catching something
    that has just fallen.

34. Wearing your favourite old jeans.

35. Cutting food into thin slices.

36. The genuine sympathy you
    feel for the motorist who
    has left their lights on.

37. Seeing someone you love
    in different clothes.

38. How all the motorists behave when
    there is a police car around.

39. The way people helpfully
    give directions.

40. Looking at a newspaper that
    someone else is reading.

41. After deciding that you are
    too ill to go to work.

42. Accelerating after the
    traffic jam has ended.

43. The way small children skip
    along as they walk.

44. Snowmen.

45. Going shopping in an area
    where you used to live.

46. The jam at the centre
    of the doughnut.

47. Picking up recently
    developed photos.

48. Mirrors that enable you to see
    the back and side of your head.

49. Convex mirrors.

50. Watching the hammers on a piano.

51. Finding even a small amount
    of money in the street.

52. Running a stick along a railing.

53. The feel of a chestnut in your hand.

54. Making someone laugh.

55. Someone holding the lift
    doors open for you.

56. Looking through binoculars
    the wrong way round.

57. Little propellers that
    turn in the wind.

58. Filling the salt cellar.

59. Swings.

60. When the lights go down
    in the cinema.

61. Sorting out the clothes that
    you don't have to iron.

62. An echo.

63. People who sing while they work.

64. Tablecloths.

65. Looking at your reflection
    in the back of a spoon.

66. When the sun suddenly comes out.

67. Watching your car in a carwash.

68. Candlelight.

69. Waking up and seeing the sky.

70. Starting a new book.

71. The last few pages of a good book.

72. The minutes directly before meeting someone you love.

73. Listening to a polite lie.

74. The sudden aroma of freshly ground coffee.

75. The smell of new furniture.

76. The bus arriving at the same time you reach the stop.

77. Squirrels.

78. Train timetable noticeboards consisting of little flaps that "flutter" when the programme changes.

79. Twirling an umbrella to get rid of the raindrops.

80. Lifting your feet off the pedals
    when cycling through a puddle.

81. Typex.

82. Those machines that blow
    the leaves away.

83. Floors that suddenly rise and
    fall, like in a cinema or theatre.

84. The sizzle you hear when you
    put something in a pan.

85. Watching cream being mixed.

86. Licking the cooking bowl.

87. Those things with a rubber blade
    that you use for cleaning windows.

88. Watching someone mop a dirty floor.

89. Teapots that pour nicely.

90. Looking at someone else's
    book or CD collection.

91. Putting your feet on the table.

92. Flopping down on a sofa.

93. The smell of children coming
    in from the fresh air.

94. Children's necks.

95. Someone thinking the same
    thing as you at the same time.

96. Meeting someone you know
    in a place that you didn't
    expect to see them.

97. Finding old letters in your desk.

98. The radio playing a song
    that was on your mind.

99. Finishing a crossword puzzle.

100. Noticing that your houseplants
     have suddenly recovered.

Gentil 13.

1. New socks.

2. Admiring a newly rearranged room.

3. Looking in an Atlas at strange, faraway places and imagining what it's like there.

4. Sitting down with a fresh cup of coffee and phoning a friend.

5. Suddenly deciding to walk more slowly.

6. Looking up at a bird in a tree and imagining how you appear from its perspective.

7. Sharing an umbrella.

8. Peeling a thick-skinned orange.

9. Sun glistening on the water.

10. Finding out the real
    names of film stars.

11. That song that makes
    you want to dance.

12. Taking a slightly different route.

13. How swans turn to face
    their attackers.

14. Cooking up something you
    haven't eaten for ages.

15. Turning the picture calender
    page over to a new month.

16. Walking around inside
    an empty church.

17. Playing with the wax
    dripping from a candle.

18. Bookmarkers.

19. Lighthouses.

20. Seeing two people enthusiastically greeting each other.

21. Going to sleep over a book.

22. Hair falling over someone's face.

23. Seeing someone in a car the same model and colour as one you used to drive.

24. The way spoked wheels in motion seem to move backwards.

25. Exotic number plates on cars.

26. Drinking out of a nice cup.

27. Getting another squeeze out of the almost empty tube of toothpaste.

28. The morning odour of bathroom ablutions.

29. Sliding down the bannisters.

30. Talking about a fine, subtle feeling to a friend who enthusiastically agrees.

31. Trees bending on a windy day.

32. Big tables.

33. Aerial photos.

34. Garden centres.

35. An avenue of trees.

36. Looking at the information on a package in different languages.

37. Unintentionally amusing translations of instructions.

38. Sand running through an hourglass.

39. Seeing someone famous in real life for the first time.

40. Wrapping a blanket around yourself.

41. Nightswimming.

42. A good cry.

43. When all the pidgeons take off around you.

44. Pictures of famous people when they were young.

45. The doorbell of an old shop.

46. The temperature suddenly rising after a cool morning.

47. Buying the CD version of a favourite LP.

48. Seeing a place you know in a movie.

49. Neon signs that"move".

50. Little free sample bottles of perfume.

51. Dogs howling outside a butcher's shop.

52. A photo of someone you like, which was taken before you got to know them.

53. A friend removing an insect from your shoulder or hair and not telling you what it was.

54. An old woman asking you to reach her something from a high supermarket shelf.

55. Film of old buildings or factory
    chimneys being blown up.

56. Speakers' corner.

57. The baton change in a relay race.

58. Letting yourself get wet in the rain.

59. Doing something with your
    other hand for a change.

60. Writing the name of
    the one you love.

61. The little titles that people
    give to their emails.

62. How kids on a plane or bus look
    at you over the back of the seat.

63. Bridges.

64. Low window sills that you can sit on.

65. When you're lost, suddenly seeing
    the sign for the motorway.

66. Seeing illuminated patterns
    when your eyes are closed.

67. Not checking the bicycle puncture repair patch too thoroughly.

68. Using a phrase or expression that your parents used to use.

69. Picking up a friend at the airport.

70. Being picked up by a friend at the airport.

71. The day you walk down the street and find that the building site has gone.

72. When someone lets you in in traffic.

73. Shopping in a foreign supermarket.

74. Vintage cars.

75. Going to sleep when it's still light.

76. Looking at people and trying to work out what their job is.

77. Finally finding out the name of a piece of music you've liked for a long time.

78. When the hangover begins to recede.

79. Looking into other people's supermarket trolleys and guessing what they're going to cook.

80. Butterflies.

81. The stretching exercises joggers do before starting.

82. People speaking French.

83. A beautiful song in a language you don't understand.

84. When someone burps and speaks at the same time and a totally different voice comes out.

85. The way children immediately convert sofas and beds into trampolines.

86. Sitting at the top of a stepladder.

87. Domino bricks.

88. Swimmers' shoulders.

89. Watching a good swimmer.

90. Reading a newspaper over breakfast.

91. Closing your eyes and gently pressing the towel against your eye sockets.

92. Drinking the sweetened milk after you've eaten the cornflakes.

93. The names of paint colours.

94. The way people hold out their hand palm upwards to see if it has started raining.

95. Glass prisms that diffuse the light into different colours.

96. The sound of a train in the distance.

97. Unusual collective names given for groups of animals.

98. Sunbeams through the trees.

99. People writing on their hands in order to remember something.

100. Those little glass domes with imitation snow in them.

DENTILS

Dentil 1.

1. Walking behind someone who's smoking.

2. When the supermarket changes everything around.

3. Walking over a freshly mopped floor.

4. In a hurry and finding yourself walking about twenty metres behind someone you don't want to talk to.

5. Crumbs.

6. When the place you want to find on the map is exactly at the edge of the page.

7. Creaking telephone box doors that take an eternity to close.

8. People who needlessly press buttons four or five times.

9. People who trip over their own feet, and then stop and stare accusingly at the pavement.

10. Humming a song you really hate.

11. Standing on something wet in your socks.

12. Slow-motion film of a crash test.

13. Machines that require the exact change.

14. Flies.

15. Not being able to find the line on a roll of sellotape.

16. Tight bottle tops.

17. Difficult-to-peel, thin-skinned oranges.

18. The supermarket trolley with the wonky wheel.

19. People who park their trolley right in front of the food displays.

20. Red-eyed photos.

21. The price tag that only half peels off.

22. Electric drills.

23. When the car mechanic breathes in sharply and rolls his eyes.

24. Taking off your trousers and then being unable to find the tracksuit bottoms that you wanted to change into.

25. The other queue that seems to be moving quicker.

26. The coins that simply drop through the machine.

27. Large cutlery.

28. Car alarms.

29. The almost indecipherable writing on lightbulbs.

30. Trying to get a cork back
    into the bottle.

31. That moment when you realize
    that you've drunk too much.

32. Parents who talk too
    much to their kids.

33. Being with a couple who
    are not getting on.

34. Buying a present and then not
    wanting to give it away.

35. Road tankers.

36. Noticing that someone you
    dislike actually has friends.

37. Toilet cubicles where the
    partitions don't reach the floor.

38. Mirrors in harshly lit bathrooms
    that make you look ill.

39. People who (hand)write in books.

40. Artificial air fresheners.

41. Putting on your T-shirt backwards.

42. When someone tells you in
the middle of the day that
your pullover is inside out.

43. A bad eraser.

44. Hard-leaded pencils.

45. An unsuccessful attempt at
sounding cheerful by saying good
morning in a high-pitched voice.

46. The phone ringing just as you're
about to open the door to leave.

47. People who sit with their chair
pushed out from the table
and their bum perched on
the edge, thus taking up an
enormous amount of room.

48. Trying on new shoes and then
seeing your old shoes beside them.

49. The waft of the garbage truck.

50. Drumming fingers.

51. Suddenly realizing that you're driving behind a hearse.

52. Channel surfers.

53. Discarded pieces of wool that momentarily look like horrible insects.

54. Horrible insects.

55. Anything that has more than four legs.

56. When a saucepan lid falls, and then spins on the ground for an extraordinarily long time making a deafening noise.

57. When the peeling of an egg goes horribly wrong because it hasn't been boiled long enough.

58. Hearing the person in the adjacent toilet cubicle.

59. Returning a stranger's friendly wave only to find that they were beckoning someone standing behind you.

60. Bad biros.

61. Someone giving you an important number over the telephone and your pen doesn't work.

62. The sound of music mixing with an ambulance siren.

63. People who hang their bag on the back of a chair, which then tips over as soon as you even brush against it.

64. The disappointing illusion that the train you're on is departing, but it's actually the train beside you.

65. The strange, fixed smile of a person holding their head to the side in order to receive a kiss on the cheek.

66. The written claim on a tube of adhesive listing the materials that it will stick, whereas, in actual fact, it only effectively glues paper together.

67. Sitting at a window seat on a plane and watching the wing vibrate.

68. When the water from a running tap hits an upturned spoon in the sink and the water splashes everywhere.

69. Turning to the next page only to find that the story ended on the previous one.

70. The music box classical music that is played while you're kept waiting on the phone.

71. Overlong answering machines.

72. People who keep repeating the punch line in an attempt to stretch the joke out.

73. Tongue twisters.

74. Caterwauling.

75. Mime artists.

76. A type of juggling, whereby the artist tries to keep lots of plates spinning on the tops of rods.

77. That moment two minutes into your journey when you realize what you've forgotten.

78. Lying about the CD or book that a friend enthusiastically lent you.

79. Being near a truck which is carrying a cargo of long metal gas bottles that look like bombs.

80. Wishing someone all the best in a new venture, but deep down being jealous.

81. Starting to cook something on a Sunday then realizing that you are out of an important ingredient.

82. Shopping in a supermarket and finding that the main thing you came for isn't there.

83. Fantastically magnified pictures
    of some horrible organism
    that lives on your skin.

84. The irresistible urge to stare at
    something horrible or disgusting.

85. Dog owners looking at
    their dog shitting.

86. Shirt labels that scratch your neck.

87. Pointless world records, like
    sitting on a pole for ages.

88. A sticky table.

89. When your foot goes to sleep.

90. Dead hands in the morning.

91. The strange annoyance that a
    badly parked car creates.

92. Hitting your "funny bone".

93. The reluctance of the
    cyclist to dismount.

94. Talking vigorously into the phone and then realizing that you're speaking to the answering machine.

95. Leaving a clear and concise message on an answering machine and then hearing the beep that indicates that you can start speaking.

96. When the time allotted for your message on an answering machine runs out in mid-sentence.

97. Crooked wheelcaps that give the illusion that the wheel is about to fall off.

98. A broken and discarded toy.

99. Thinking about something you didn't buy and should have.

100. Microphone testing.

Dentil 2.

1. Household product containers that are so artistically designed that you can't work out how to open them.

2. Shopping television.

3. Coat hangers used as car antennas.

4. Alsatian dogs.

5. When the bottom half of your dunked biscuit falls into your tea.

6. Shaking a blanket in the sunlight and then realizing how much dust there is in the world.

7. The way time just disappears when you're trying to get ready in the morning.

8. The things people believe.

9.   Our shameful fascination
     with natural disasters.

10. When someone you don't
     know well enough has a piece
     of food stuck to their face.

11. When you have to admit to yourself
     that you're annoyed at the two old
     people who are getting in your way.

12. When someone curtly tells you
     on the phone that they are too
     busy, leaving you wondering
     why they answered at all.

13. The rubbish people talk.

14. Small people with big dogs.

15. Abandoned car batteries.

16. The guilty feeling when
     finding something that was
     misplaced after having suspected
     someone of stealing it.

17. Electric organs.

18. When practically bald people
    brush the last remaining
    strands over their head.

19. Getting ready to leave the house
    and then half an hour later
    you still haven't done it.

20. Anything that features
    chimpanzees with clothes on.

21. Being unable to find the light switch
    in someone else's bathroom.

22. The bareness of a room after the
    decorations have been taken down.

23. The grumpy dog-owner look
    that tells you that you will be to
    blame if the dog attacks you.

24. Butter straight from the
    fridge that won't spread.

25. When someone tries to convince
    you that you're in bad form.

26. Sitting on the toilet and
    realizing that the seat is up,
    or worse, there isn't one.

27. Something you lent to someone
    years ago that you never got
    back and it still niggles you.

28. The little red "Pull" attachment
    that comes off in your fingers
    instead of opening the package.

29. Having to bend down
    to tie a shoelace.

30. Sun-studio tans.

31. A hairstyle that sadly dates someone.

32. The memory of something you lost
    and never knew what happened to it.

33. When acquaintances that you
    always knew as a couple, break up.

34. When a person holds a piece of paper in one hand, and then hits it with the back of their other hand, indicating that it's the news they've been waiting for.

35. A part of a street that you don't like and you're not sure why.

36. Deciding, out of politeness, to let someone tell you a joke that you've already heard.

37. Smiling and sighing at a hopelessly out-of-date joke.

38. Jeans that have been cut so short that the pocket linings show below the edge.

39. A person who repeats a verbal slip that you made in order to highlight it.

40. A place that seems pleasant enough, but which you know would be frightening in the dark.

41. The sad clang of a stringed
    instrument that has just fallen
    over or been bumped into.

42. When someone widens their eyes and
    sings a song into your face in order
    to convince you that you know it.

43. Getting your hands soapy and then
    not being able to turn off the tap.

44. People with an ordinary-sounding
    name, but which is spelt differently,
    and who get irritated with
    others who don't know this.

45. People who insist on being
    addressed by their academic title.

46. When the shop assistant serves you
    without speaking or looking at you.

47. Discovering a discoloured
    bruise on your leg and not
    knowing where it came from.

48. Soft, wrinkled skin after having
    been in the bath too long.

49. Realizing that you're being deliberately kept waiting.

50. Cutting bread with the wrong knife because you can't find the proper one.

51. Going indoors after being in the bright sun and finding it hard to see anything.

52. Vegans.

53. How your hair looks after you've put on your pullover.

54. Someone tickling you when you don't want it.

55. Trying to do something quietly and ending up making a huge amount of noise.

56. Thoughtfully putting a pencil in your mouth and then discovering that someone else has already been chewing it.

57. Those stupid names that media celebrities give their children.

58. A book that has got wet.

59. Being caught talking to yourself.

60. People who put burnt matches back into the matchbox.

61. Frequently running into someone you don't especially like because you have similar routines.

62. Seldom running into someone you like because your routines are different.

63. Those mad people who shout in the street.

64. Car horns.

65. Namedroppers.

66. Sneezing.

67. People who sneeze deliberately loudly.

68. An unsuccessful attempt
    to contain a sneeze.

69. When a person refers to their
    favourite rock star by surname only.

70. After unpacking your shopping,
    finding that you have bought
    the low-calorie or diabetic
    version of something.

71. When one member of a couple
    angers and embarrasses the other by
    crossing the road without them.

72. People who beep their
    horns in traffic jams.

73. People who accuse you of
    giving them a cold.

74. Someone putting their hands
    over your eyes so that you
    have to guess who it is.

75. Seeing souvenirs that are exactly
    the same in different countries.

76. An old couple being rude and impatient with each other.

77. When your "Real Ireland" postcard has "Made in Portugal" printed on it.

78. Something made of plastic and metal that you put in the normal rubbish bin, because you simply don't know what to do with it.

79. Wigs that look like wigs.

80. Licking stamps.

81. Long dog leads.

82. When you touch someone or something and there's a discharge of static electricity through your finger.

83. The unfairness of the phrase"Get a life".

84. The names of famous prisons.

85. The undeniable excitement of military hardware.

86. Re-reading a book years later
    and being disappointed.

87. A pop song you once liked
    but now find ridiculous.

88. Being near a truck that's emptying
    glass-recycling containers.

89. Blowing up balloons.

90. The thick, double windows of an
    underground train that make you
    look exhausted and translucent.

91. The front hotplate on the
    cooker that gets especially dirty
    because you use it so much.

92. A wedding entourage beeping
    their horns while driving
    through the streets.

93. People who hit the enter button
    on their PCs aggressively.

94. Driving through an extremely dark
    tunnel and then realizing that you're
    still wearing your dark glasses.

95. People who forget to take
    off their crash helmets.

96. People who wear dark
    glasses indoors.

97. A household article that never
    really finds a "home"and has to be
    looked for everytime you want it.

98. People who jog in a busy
    shopping street.

99. Hiccups.

100. An acquaintance whose name
     you constantly get wrong.

Dentil 3.

1. When your joints make
   a snapping noise.

2. Suddenly groping yourself because
   you think you've forgotten your keys.

3. An old trailer of a film that
   subsequently flopped.

4. About to curl up and you
   can't find your book.

5. A large pane of glass attached
   to the side of a glazier's van.

6. Hyenas.

7. When one end of the waistcord
   of your tracksuit bottoms
   slips inside the material.

8. That feeling of being cheated when you find that one, or even more, of the eggs has broken in the egg box.

9. Discarded photo snaps.

10. Someone, although a nice enough sort of person, who gets on your nerves.

11. Accidentally taking a gulp of someone else's coffee.

12. When the escalator doesn't work.

13. When someone starts to sing the song that you were happily humming to yourself.

14. When the strip of sellotape that you want to use folds over and sticks irretrievably to itself.

15. When the belt doesn't have enough holes.

16. The alarming amount of hairs left in the sink after you've washed your hair.

17. Having to look for something you
    had in your hand thirty seconds ago.

18. A small crack in a beautiful glass.

19. When you haven't got a
    coin for the trolley.

20. When a newspaper runs an
    April fool joke and you feel so
    gullible for having fallen for it.

21. When a racehorse crosses
    the finish line riderless.

22. When an acquaintance
    enthusiastically approaches
    you and you're mortified,
    because you've just farted.

23. Sugar dispensers.

24. When you leave something
    on the roof of the car.

25. When the through train goes
    thundering past the platform.

26. Sales letters with a fake printed signature.

27. A knot in the wood just where you want to screw something in.

28. A suntan only on the lower arms and neck.

29. The slightly inadequate feeling you get when someone announces sprightly that they get up at 5.   30.   every morning, including weekends.

30. Burning your tongue on a hot drink.

31. People who stand on motorway bridges.

32. A pullover tucked inside the trousers.

33. The apparent slowness of a low-flying passenger plane when seen from the ground.

34. Whistles.

35. Whistling kettles.

36. Whistling people.

37. When you tell a joke
    and nobody gets it.

38. When someone lets you tell half
    the joke and then interrupts
    with the punch line.

39. When someone asks you to repeat
    something that you don't want
    to because you have already
    discarded it as unimportant.

40. Foreign male tourists who
    get killed or injured at the
    bull run in Pamplona.

41. Men mobile phoning their
    partner from the supermarket
    because they can't make up
    their mind about something.

42. The price of an item that's been crossed out and the new lower price written on, but, on closer inspection, you see that the whole thing is printed.

43. A kid that you can clearly see is looking for something to break and the parents are ignoring it.

44. Airily walking through the aisles of the supermarket trying to disguise the fact that you've lost your trolley.

45. People with a towel around them trying to change into a swimming costume.

46. Trying to behave naturally in the presence of someone famous.

47. Large, curving skid marks on the motorway.

48. The soggy tissue in the pocket of something that has just been washed.

49. People who jump out of their
     cars to fetch something and
     leave the motor running.

50. Guiltily having a pee
     while swimming.

51. Having two words in your mind
     but only wanting to say one, then
     speaking a hybrid of the two.

52. How everyone tells lies, yet become
     indignant when accused of it.

53. A shredded tyre by the roadside.

54. People who try to impress you by
     citing how little time it took them
     to drive from one place to another.

55. Personalized car number plates.

56. Being the only person at
     a country bus stop

57. People who stir their tea and
     then put the wet spoon directly
     back into the sugar bowl.

58. Clotted soap dishes.

59. A word you've always mispronounced.

60. When the hairdresser uses a cut-throat razor to scrape the back of your neck.

61. The name"Cut-throat razor".

62. A real handkerchief that's been used.

63. When a person refers you to a document rather than give you the information verbally.

64. Electric coffee grinders.

65. Quicksand.

66. The telephone number of a local government office that no one ever answers.

67. The tinkle of a coin dropping on the ground.

68. People who crack their knuckles.

69. Looking into your hanky.

70. Large, theatrical moustaches.

71. When you suddenly think
    that a familiar word seems
    to be spelt wrongly.

72. The bug-eyed way some adults feel
    they have to talk to children.

73. People who tap animal cages to
    get the creature's attention.

74. A crooked toupee.

75. A persistent fly.

76. Bad hair days.

77. When the toilet is occupied.

78. When you try to take an
    egg out of the egg box and
    it breaks in your fingers.

79. A rumbling tummy.

80. Standing barefoot on a lego brick.

81. When a drawer sticks because
    something inside is blocking it.

82. Developing an inexplicable
    dislike of an actor or singer.

83. Flightless birds.

84. A fat face in which you can see
    the thinner one it used to be.

85. People who tell off their dogs.

86. Pouring a fizzy drink
    that then overflows.

87. The spider in the bathroom.

88. A creaky bed.

89. Members of the public on a TV show
    who look like members of the public.

90. A person standing on a second-
    storey window sill cleaning
    the open window.

91. A doormat with the
    word"Welcome"on it.

92. Specialized technical and medical words which you will never forget, because they caused you so much money and misery.

93. People who stand right at the roadside during a cross-country motor rally.

94. Your Swiss army knife that you never use.

95. Artificially created grill marks on packaged meat.

96. When someone remarks that the coffee tastes funny making you uncertain about your own.

97. Trying to tidy your bed while you're still lying in it.

98. Having to make the decision of where to pee outdoors.

99. Having a pee outdoors and, of course, a car comes.

100. Having to stop having a
    pee halfway through.

Dentil 4.

1.   When your car won't start
     because of a flat battery and
     suddenly your prized possession
     is turned into a heap of junk.

2.   A person with whom you share
     a mutual friend, but who you
     yourself don't particularly like.

3.   Biting into a beautiful-looking
     chocolate and then finding
     that it contains marzipan.

4.   When the large chewing-
     gum bubble bursts.

5.   When another driver flashes you
     because your lights are on full beam.

6.   Forgetting where you parked the car.

7. Seeing something that you make a
    mental note of to pick up before it
    gets lost, and then, later, not being
    able to remember where you saw it.

8. Trying to help someone look
    for something by mentioning
    that you saw it somewhere, and
    then being put under pressure
    by that person to remember.

9. A stone, firmly wedged into the sole
    of your running shoes, which then
    makes a scraping sound as you walk.

10. Receiving a holiday postcard
    which is so badly written that you
    can't work out who it's from.

11. When you uneccessarily buy
    six different postcards to send
    to six different people.

12. Looking through piles of information
    on the food packet, when all you
    want to know is how long to cook it.

13. When the mousetrap works.

14. Sudden huge, dark stains on
    the pavement indicating the
    onset of a heavy downpour.

15. The sudden buzzing noise of a fly.

16. A child with a harmonica.

17. A tourist that has to be told
    to stop eating when entering
    an ancient church.

18. Graffiti that only consists
    of someone's initials.

19. Graffiti on an old monument.

20. When an old shop closes down.

21. When there are female cleaners
    in the men's public toilet.

22. Those outdoor French toilets
    where everyone can see you.

23. Not being able to pee because there
    are people standing on each side
    of you at the adjacent urinals.

24. The way TV adverts are louder.

25. A two-hour film on TV which
    lasts three hours because
    of the advertisements.

26. Used tea bags.

27. The steep winding drive-in entrance
    to a multi-storey car park.

28. A lobster being cooked.

29. A customer in front of you taking
    ages to count out the exact money.

30. The blast of wind that hits you
    after a large vehicle flies past.

31. When the fittings in a foreign
    holiday house are the same as
    the ones you have at home.

32. Shampoo in your eyes.

33. When a dog barks at a
    handicapped person.

34. A car that can't possibly have been to Canada with a "Canada" sticker on it.

35. Car stickers with out-of-date jokes on them.

36. A small, run-over animal.

37. Wanting to spit.

38. Underground car parks.

39. Pulling up too far from the ticket dispenser at the car park and so having to get out of the car to get the ticket.

40. When the light bulb fuses.

41. The seamed part of a shirt where the buttons and buttonholes are, which folds over on itself, making it difficult to iron.

42. People who put the names of their children on their car.

43. Little cardboard pine trees
    that you hang in your car
    to make it smell better.

44. Forgetting someone's name almost
    as soon as you've heard it.

45. Swallowing a small fly.

46. A megastore with a huge sign
    above the entrance saying
    how great it is to see you.

47. When they change a shop or
    facade, how quickly you forget
    what the old one looked like.

48. A building that looks OK from
    a distance, but, on approaching,
    you discover that it's alarmingly
    run-down and abandoned.

49. The loneliness of the last stop.

50. When your lovely white shirt
    comes out of the wash…. pink.

51. A drinks bottle from which
    the label has come off.

52. Your watch with the date on it that is always wrong.

53. Modern orchestral music that sounds like a traffic jam.

54. When milk burns.

55. Quoting a proverb that casts someone in a negative light.

56. The stamped envelope in your bag that you wanted to post three days ago.

57. When you see Christmas products in the shops in September.

58. Forgetting the shopping list.

59. When you're just about to sneeze and nothing happens.

60. Getting caught in the rain when you were having a good hair day.

61. How difficult it is to estimate how many people are in a room.

62. Our Western inability to remember Arab or Oriental names.

63. The coldness of the belt buckle on your skin.

64. Having to decide whether to run for the bus or not.

65. Having to ask someone if they would like another cup of tea, but hoping they look at their watch and announce that they really must be on their way.

66. Selecting a CD from your collection, opening up the case and- there's nothing in it.

67. When you drop something and it seems to disappear, only to be found later in the most unlikely spot.

68. When the fly hits the part of the windscreen right in front of your eyes.

69. When you run out of something that
    seems to last an eternity, like salt.

70. The truck that slows everyone down.

71. Your unfair dislike of the
    driver of the truck that's
    slowing everyone down.

72. Being the driver of the truck
    that's slowing everyone down.

73. When you make far too
    much rice/noodles.

74. The coughing in the congregation.

75. The feeling of the wet shower
    curtain to your bare skin.

76. When you have trapped the spider
    between a piece of paper and a cup,
    go to throw it out, and then realize
    you have already lost it again.

77. The ridiculous misunderstandings
    you start inventing when you
    have arrived for a date and,
    after fifteen minutes, the person
    has still not turned up.

78. When everyone gets off the
    railway carriage leaving you
    alone and in doubt.

79. Documentaries about insects
    usually shown around the time
    you're having your evening meal.

80. Foreign toilets that consist of
    only an opening in the floor and
    in which you can only stand.

81. When the fat in the hot
    pan"spits"at you.

82. People who put their bag
    on the seat beside them on
    a crowded train or bus.

83. Eating a meal for the last time because you realize that you're fed up with this recipe.

84. When you can't remember which teas/coffees you put the sugar in.

85. Interrupting someone sitting on the toilet.

86. Someone telling you to be careful after you've slipped.

87. When you switch on an electrical appliance, and only half an hour later realize that it's not working because it isn't plugged in.

88. When the chalk squeaks as someone is writing on the blackboard.

89. Those crinkly shirts that are an absolute bugger to iron.

90. When you take an item off a high shelf and something else falls off as well.

91. A woman who looks attractive
    from the back but when she
    turns around is disappointing.

92. When you put too much
    cold water into the bath.

93. Someone being unnecessarily
    grumpy with you just because
    you got the wrong number.

94. Thermos flask tea.

95. When the shop assistant slaps the
    change onto the counter instead
    of giving it into your hand.

96. When you can't pick up a coin
    from a hard smooth surface.

97. Breaking a fingernail.

98. Closing the door to leave and
    then realizing that you want
    to go to the toilet again.

99. Having to ring the reception bell.

100. When you cut your finger on the edge of a piece of paper.

Dentil 5.

1. Having to turn your pullover around while you're still wearing it because it's back to front.

2. When the dog tries to shag your leg.

3. Dressing up in ridiculous layers of waterproof clothing and, just as you put your foot on the bicycle pedal, it stops raining.

4. When you forget your sandwiches.

5. A small cross with flowers marking the scene of a fatal accident.

6. When a friend gets a dreadful haircut.

7. When the train stops in the tunnel.

8. People commenting on the recent haircut that you'd already forgotten about.

9. When the camera flashes and you're sure you blinked at that moment.

10. The uncertainty of putting a letter into a remotely situated letterbox.

11. How slow a kettle seems to be when you watch it.

12. When someone relates a common falsehood to you.

13. Barbed wire.

14. Hearing your own voice on a recording.

15. Listening to someone for the umpteenth time talking about their plans.

16. Someone standing in the kitchen when you're busy.

17. When you sit down at your PC for a good evening's surfing and you can't think of anything to look up.

18. Songs that contain yodelling.

19. That plop that tells you that a bird has shit on your head.

20. Being with someone who walks really slowly.

21. Walking over a surface that makes your trainers squeak.

22. As the nail you're hammering into the wall starts to bend.

23. A caller who leaves their number on your answering machine spoken so quickly, that you have to keep replaying the message to get it down.

24. Starting your dishwasher, and then five minutes later there is a kitchen utensil in it that you really need.

25. The kitchen utensil that you
   really need, but is so stained
   that you will have to clean it.

26. The puzzled feeling you have when
   you tell a lie and you didn't need to.

27. Sleeping in.

28. Noticing that you're exaggerating.

29. When you've turned on
   the wrong hotplate.

30. Armchair critics who rail
   at the television.

31. Fast drivers.

32. Slow drivers.

33. Motorway rest areas.

34. Clothes that tell you instantly
   that a person is poor.

35. The hour you lose when
   the clocks go forward.

36. The general confusion when
the clocks go forward.

37. When an ex-friend wants
something back that was
supposed to be a present.

38. Finding your bicycle lying
on the ground.

39. When a piece of crockery
smashes in a restaurant.

40. People unfairly applauding
when a piece of crockery
smashes in a restaurant.

41. Exotic food that consists of the
part of an animal that a European
would never dream of eating.

42. Finding the second sock not long
after throwing out the first one.

43. Elvis Presley impersonators.

44. When everyone, both cars
and pedestrians, is standing
waiting at the traffic lights.

45. The tall person who decides to sit in front of you at the concert.

46. Filling up the washing machine,
putting the powder in,
setting the program and then
forgetting to switch it on.

47. When you find an item from the
deep freeze left abandoned on a
normal shelf in the supermarket.

48. Shoelaces in a knot.

49. Realizing that your shoes
are letting in water.

50. A cut on your finger that
you keep bumping.

51. When someone says they didn't
phone you because they forgot.

52. When something that used to amuse
you in a person doesn't anymore.

53. A barking dog in a parked car.

54. The unpleasant blast of the wind when you turn the corner of a high building.

55. Heavy suitcases.

56. The deep, grumbling sound of a suitcase on small wheels being pulled across a hard floor.

57. Finding a coin of low worth on the ground and having to consider the indignity of picking it up.

58. When there are not enough cornflakes in the packet to make a bowlful.

59. When someone asks you if you are asleep and you were before they asked you.

60. A limp handshake.

61. The forgotten umbrella at the bus stop.

62. When an acquaintance gives you back a long overdue, borrowed book, casually mentioning that they never got around to reading it.

63. When you find out only later that you really annoyed somebody.

64. When someone announces that they want to ask you a question and then changes their mind.

65. A shop that only opens on request.

66. When your lips stick to the paper cup.

67. When your feeling of lightness and mobility is spoiled when you realize you have forgotten your bag.

68. When a foodstuff just out of the tin briefly maintains the shape of the tin it was in.

69. A very old person stopping and leaning on something to rest.

70. Scraping dough off a big spoon with a smaller one and ending up simply transferring it from one to the other.

71. Mopping a floor clean and then discovering that there's something you need at the other end of the room.

72. The continuous blaring horn that means that someone is parked in.

73. Bicycle helmets.

74. When people you don't really know well sing "Happy Birthday " to you.

75. Ticket touts.

76. The radio part of your stereo set that you never use.

77. When someone insists that you listen to a piece of music that they love, but which you have never heard before.

78. When the bottle top won't come off.

79. When the cork in the wine bottle you're opening comes apart.

80. Standing behind someone in the bakery who wants all sorts of different things.

81. Traffic wardens.

82. Cobwebs

83. When you can't find a pin for the pinboard.

84. When the dentist tells you exactly what he is going to do.

85. Deep-sea fish.

86. People with lobster suntans.

87. When you get out of a hot bath and you're completely red from the waist down.

88. When the coin gets stuck in the supermarket trolley.

89. A slow puncture.

90. Junk mail.

91. The small drop of pee that leaks out
    and stains the front of your trousers.

92. Suddenly thinking of something
    important and witty to say
    when your mouth is full.

93. When you start singing to
    cover up the fact that you
    were talking to yourself.

94. Suddenly noticing that you
    haven't got your watch on.

95. Talking to someone who is looking
    at your chest instead of you.

96. When the toilet bowl fills
    to the brim after flushing
    because of some blockage.

97. When you put the egg into
    boiling water, and it cracks.

98. Finding that you have a photograph
    in your collection of someone
    you never really liked.

99. When you talk about a subtle, personal feeling and no one gets it.

100. The fact that you have to pay for a book subtitled: "Nice Things in Life That Don't Cost Anything".

Lightning Source UK Ltd.
Milton Keynes UK
UKOW050839291211

184484UK00001B/7/A